This book belongs to

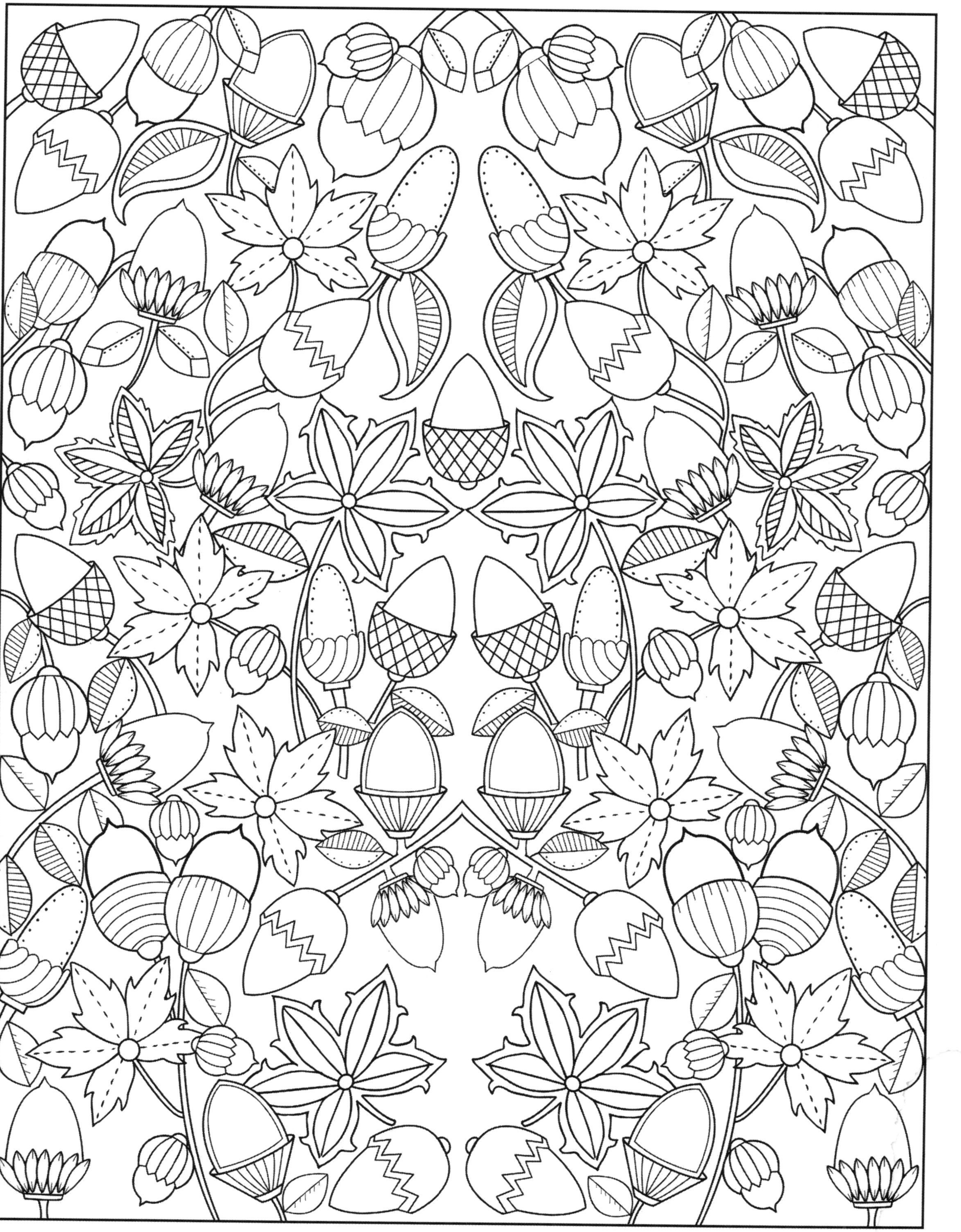

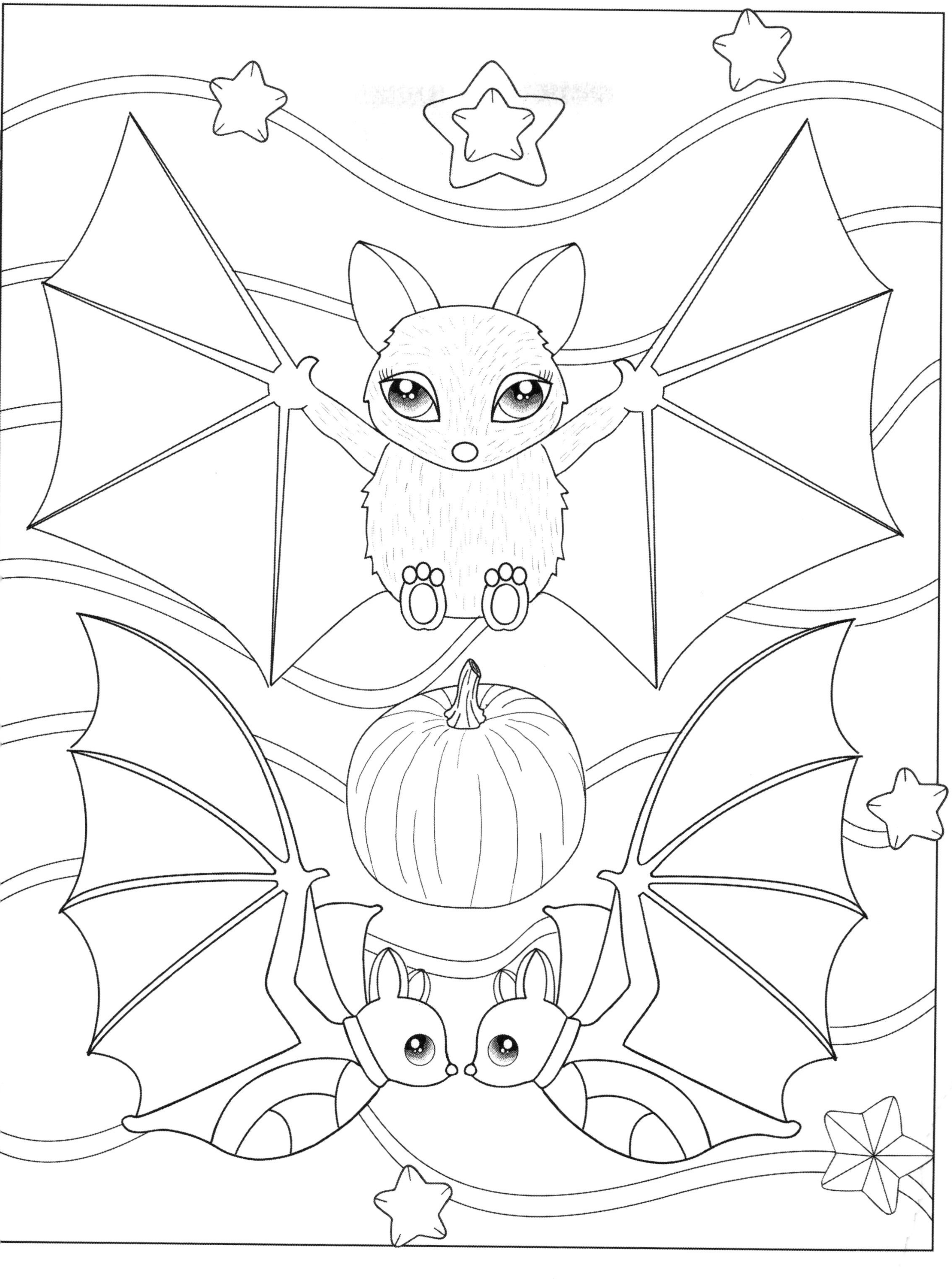

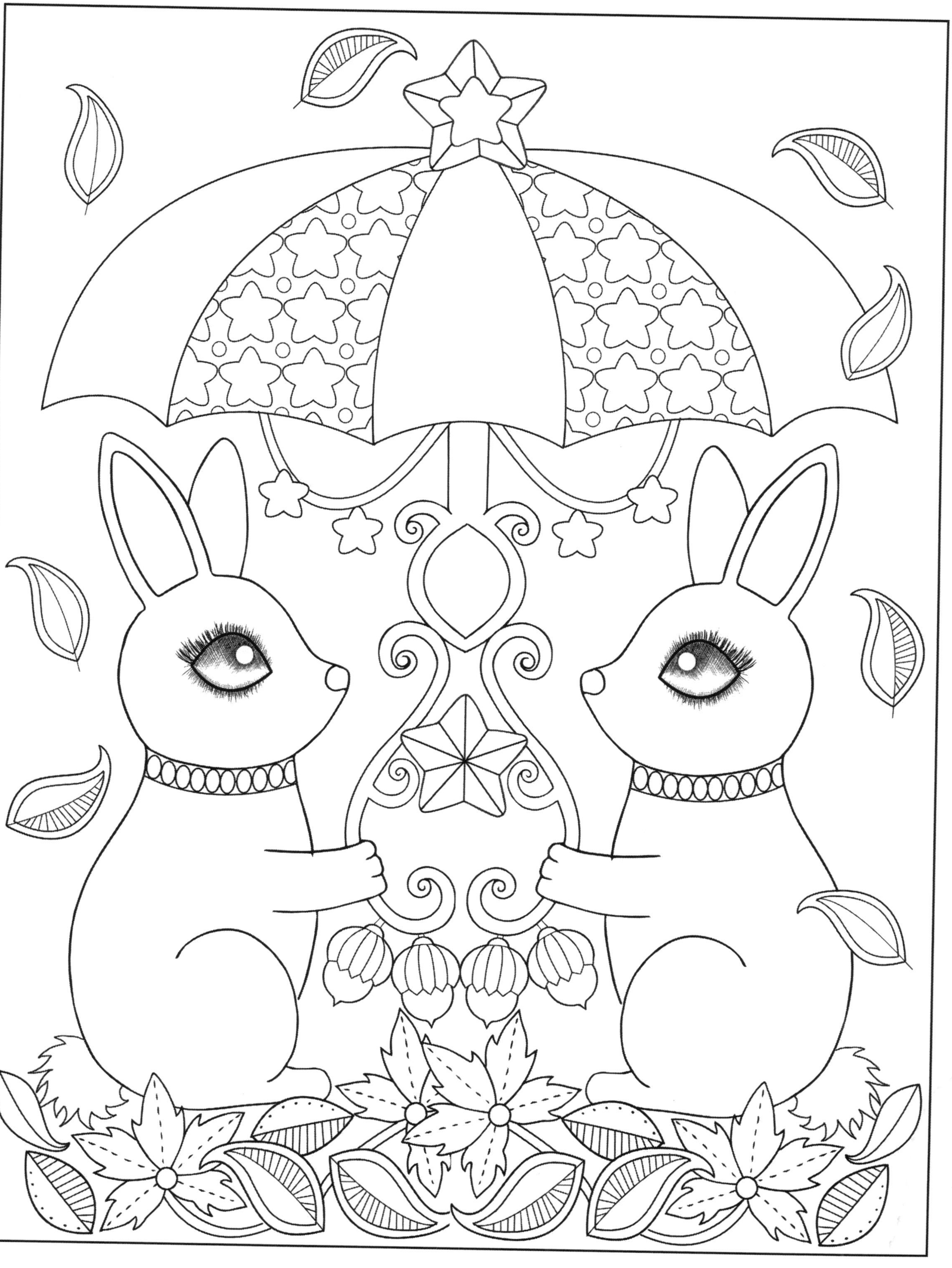

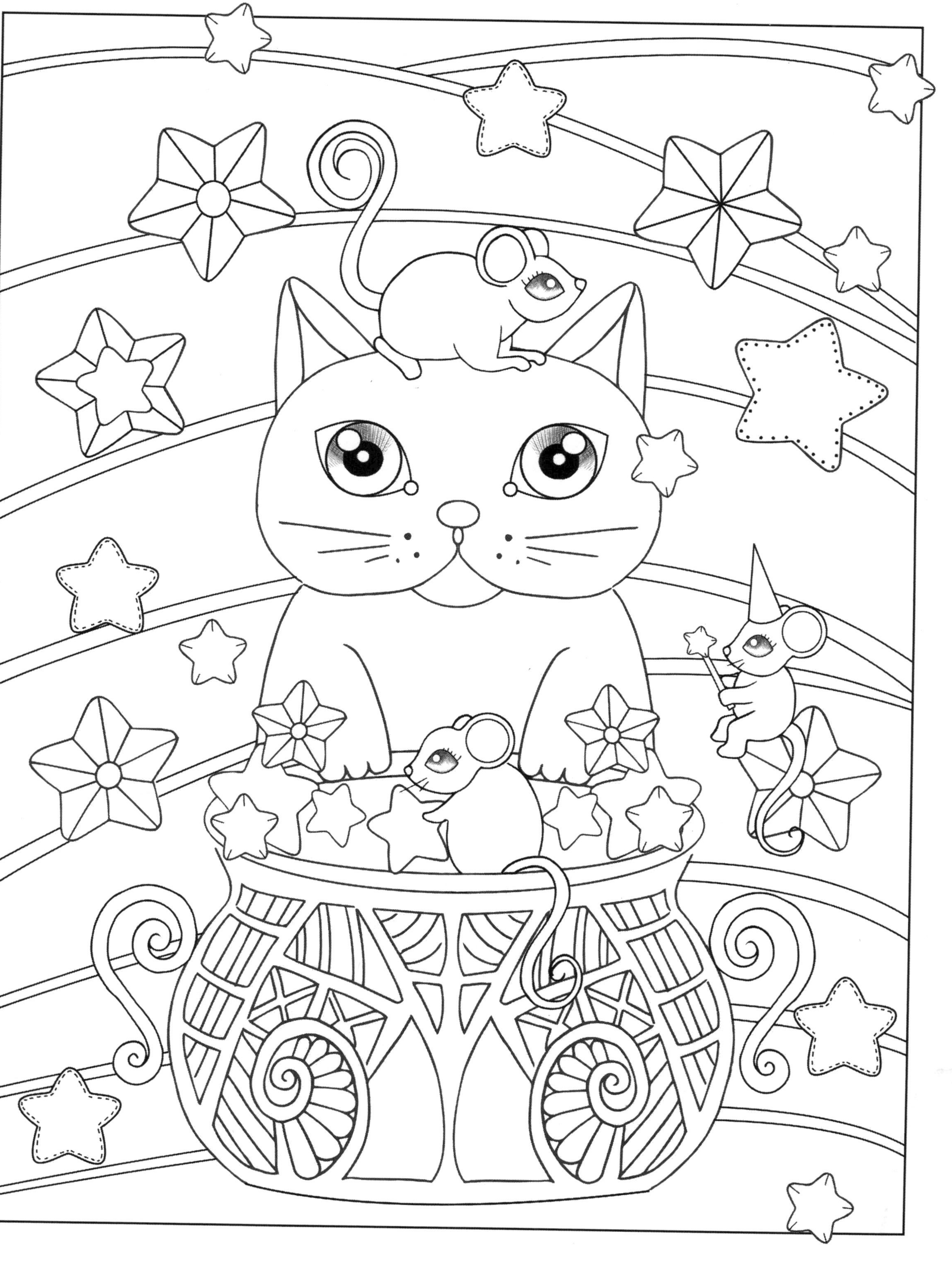

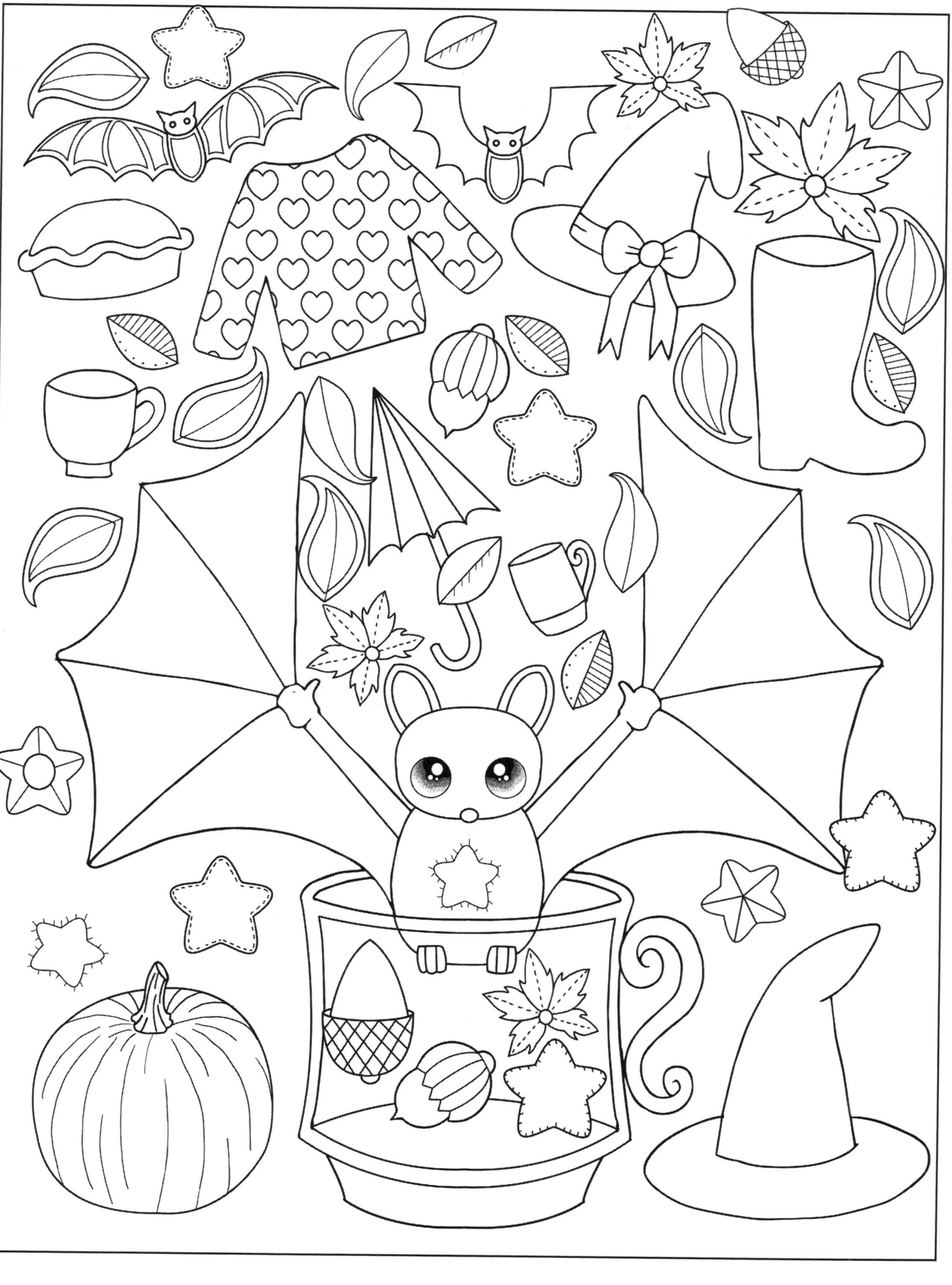

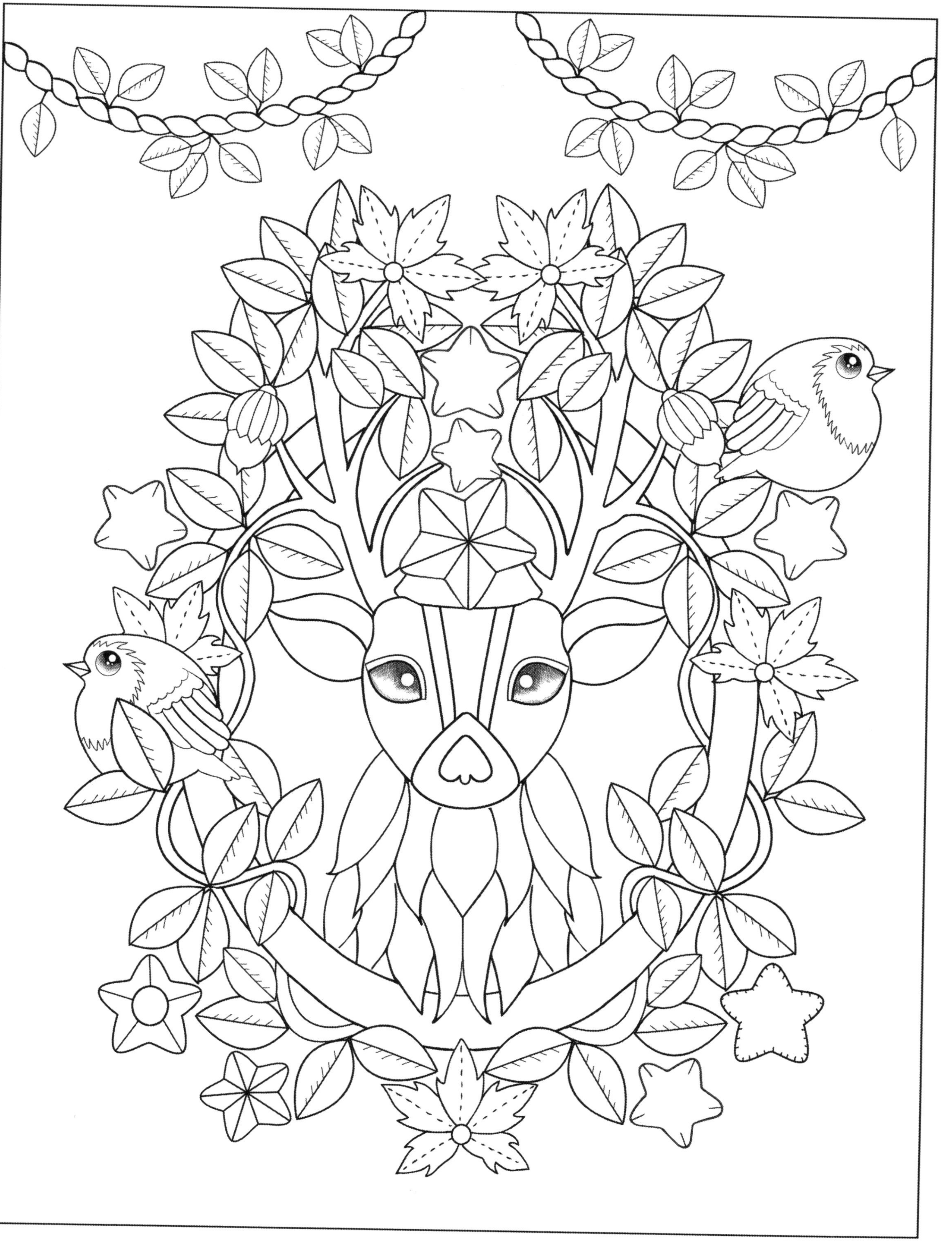

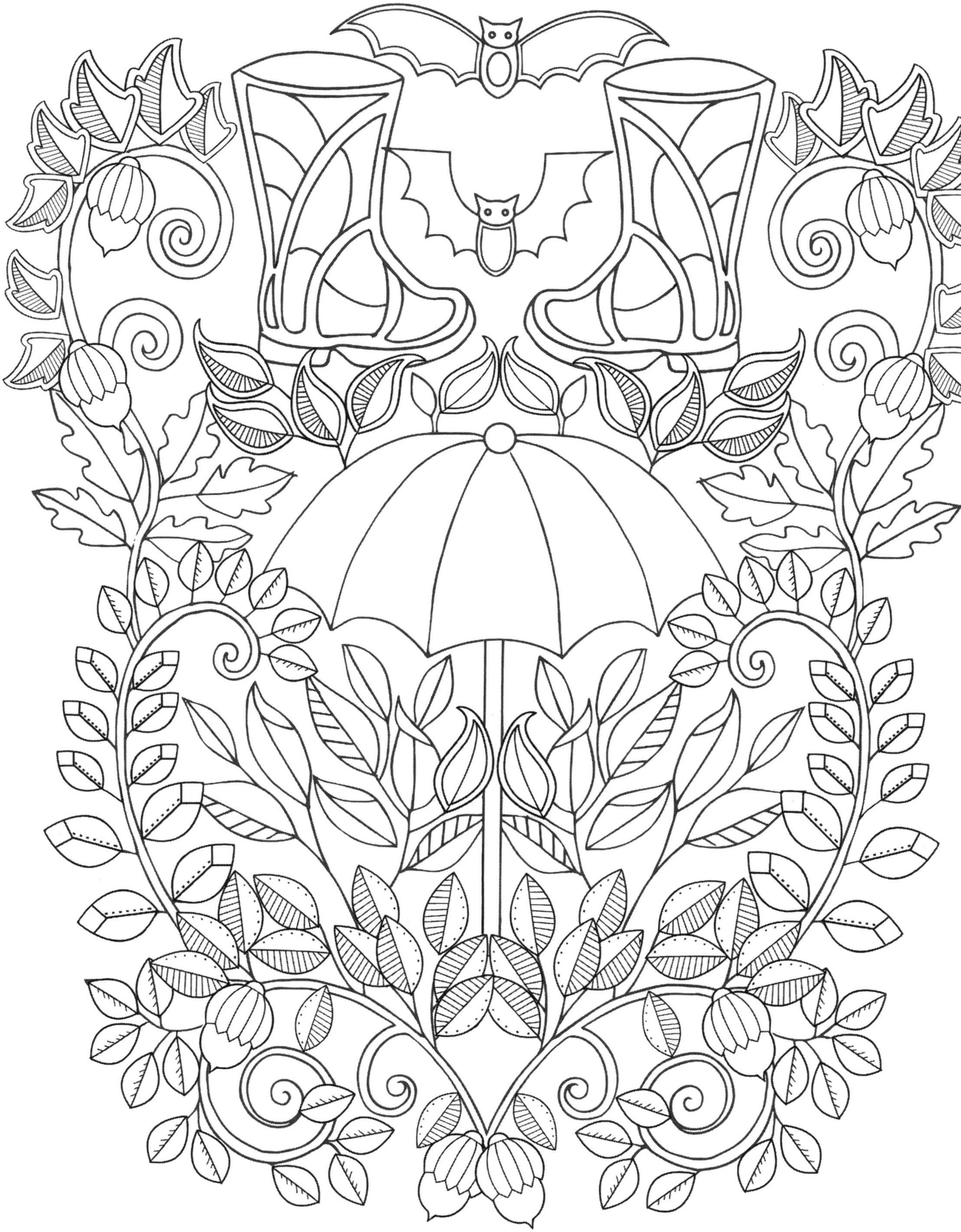

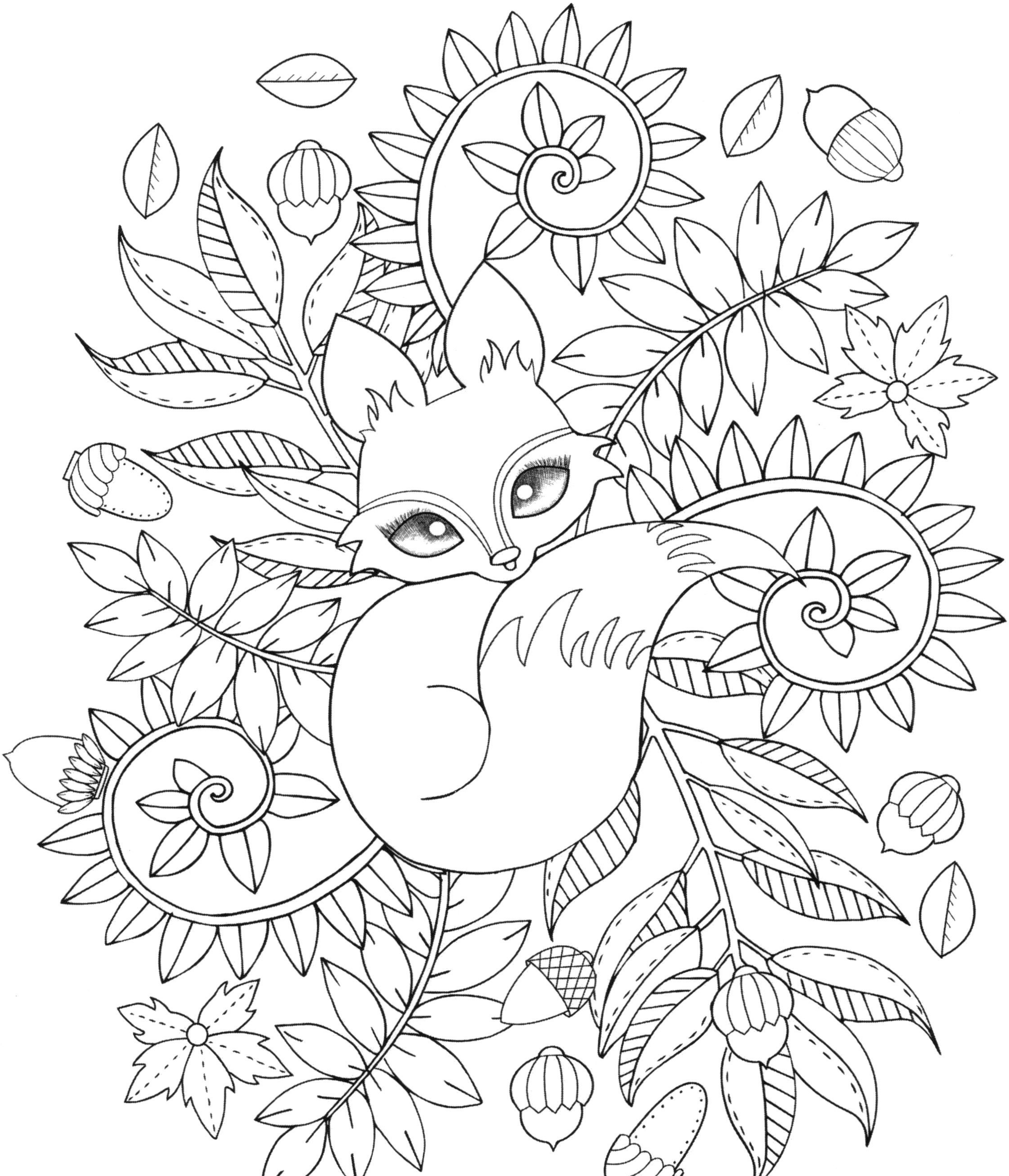

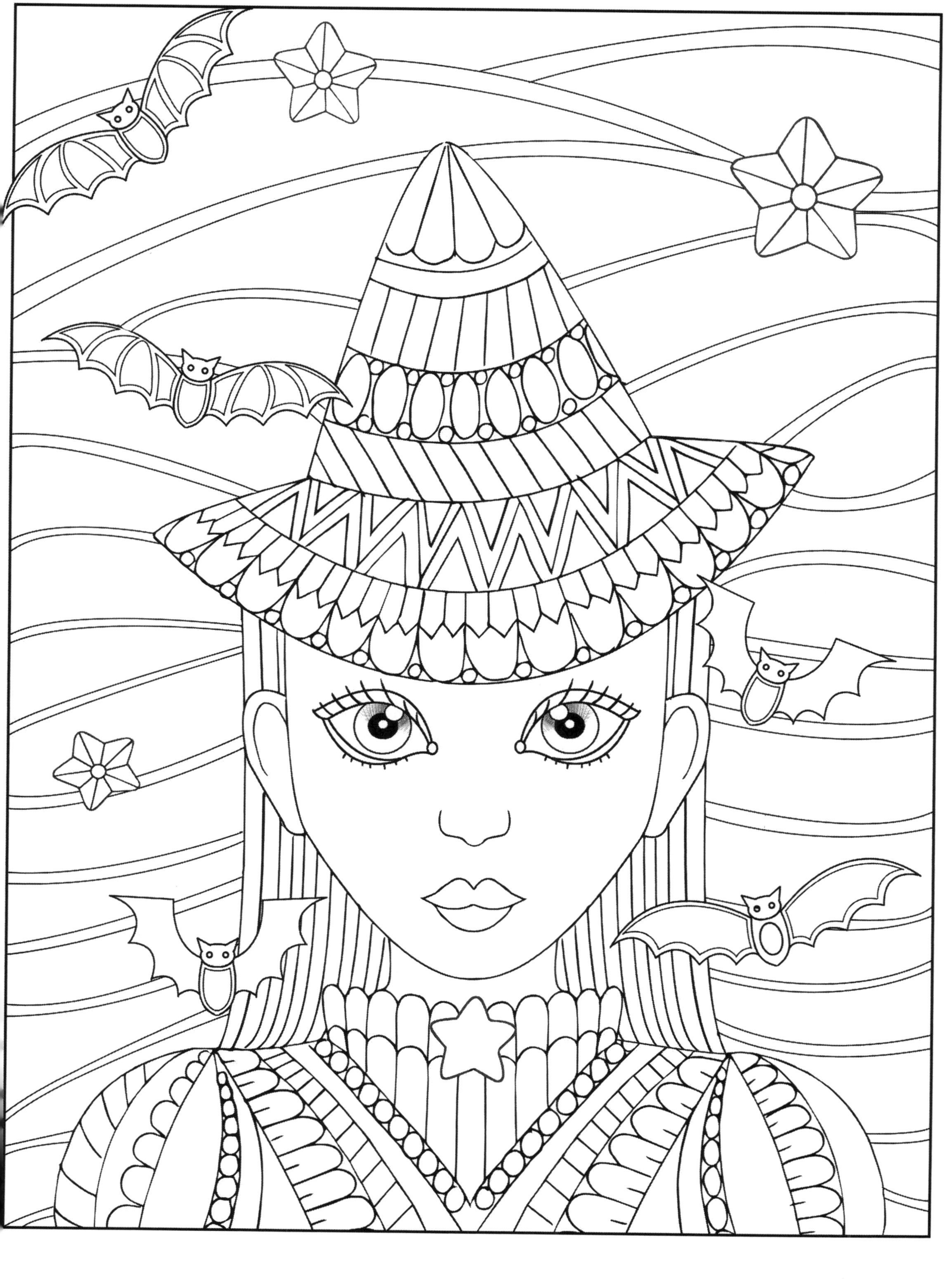

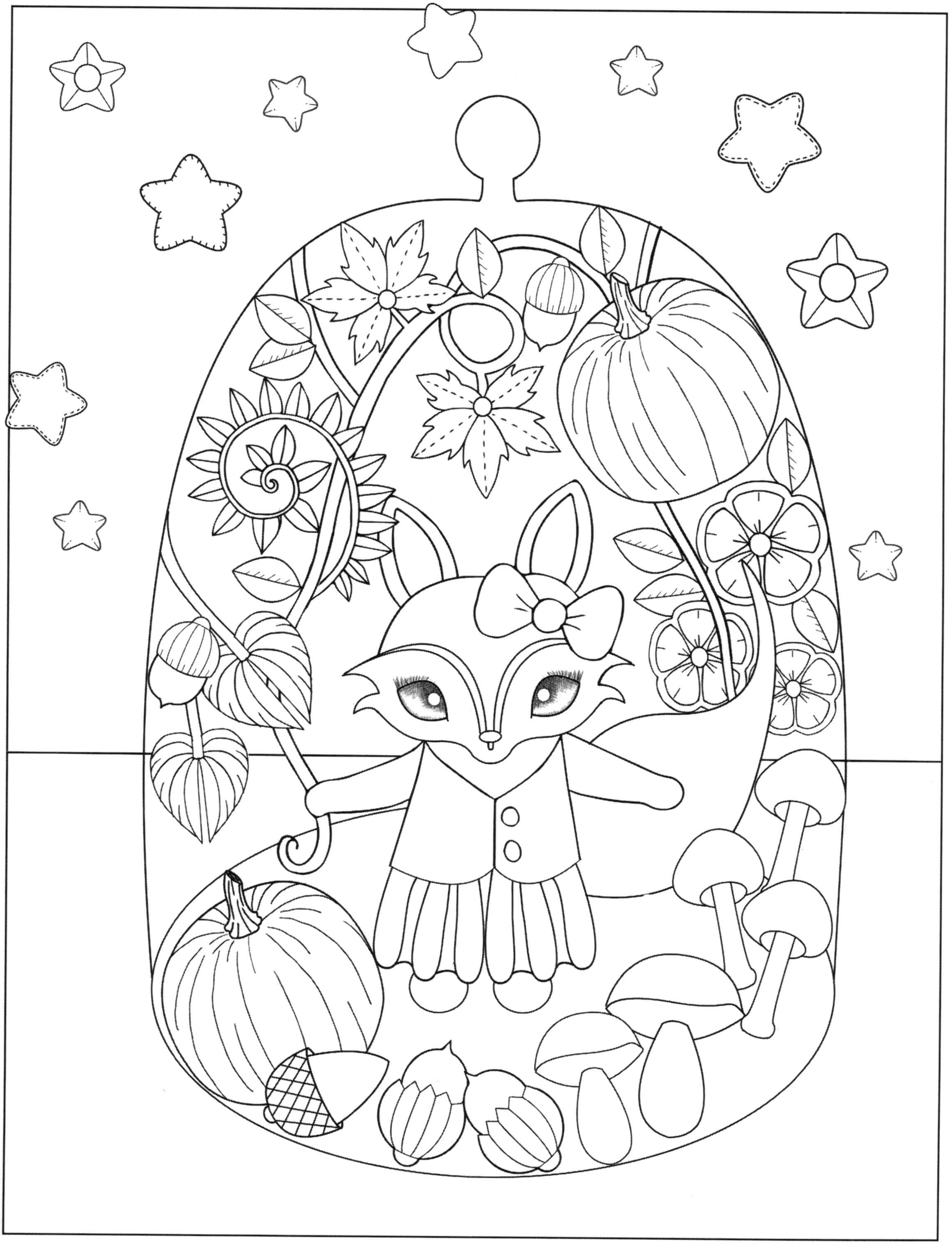

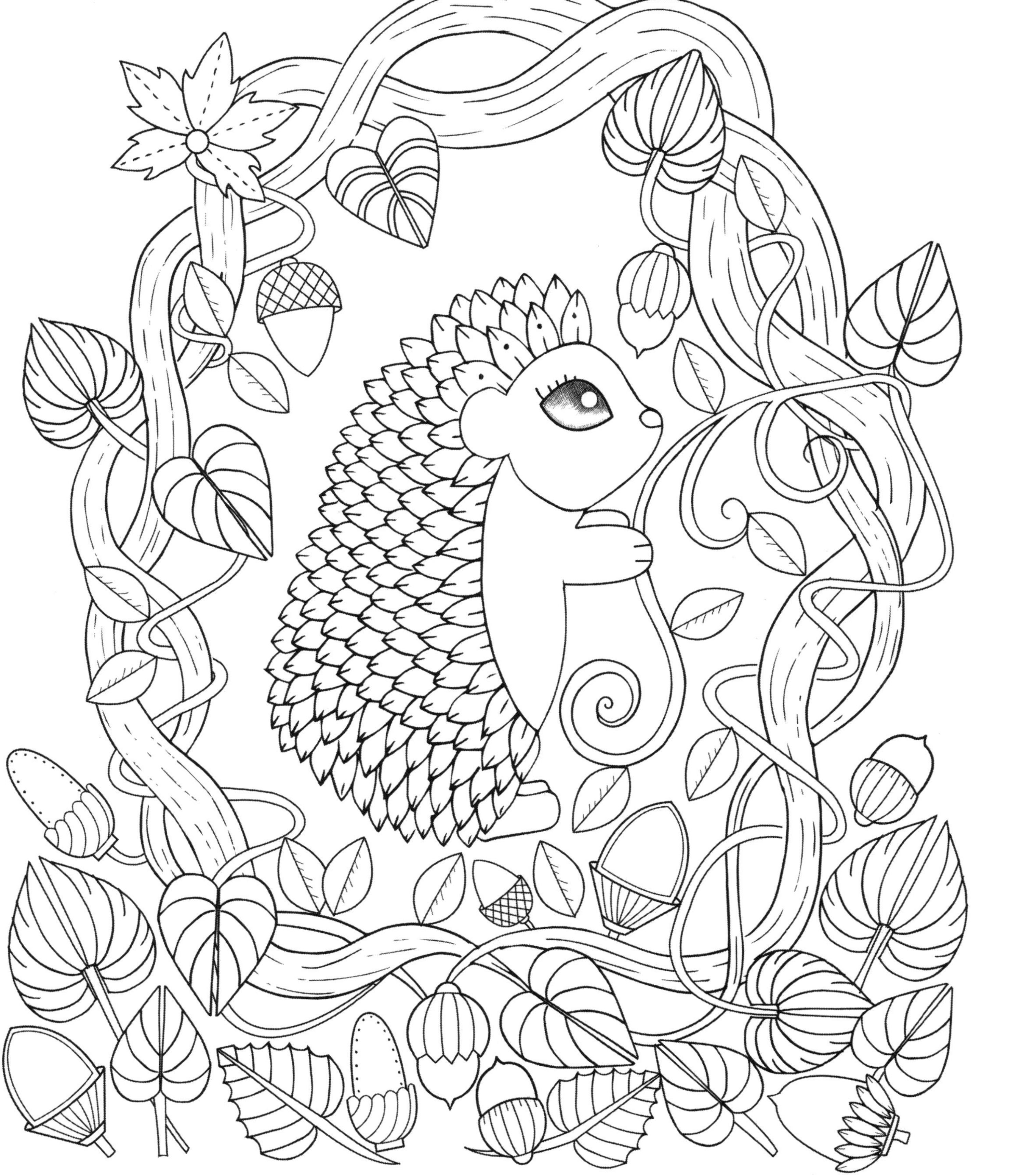

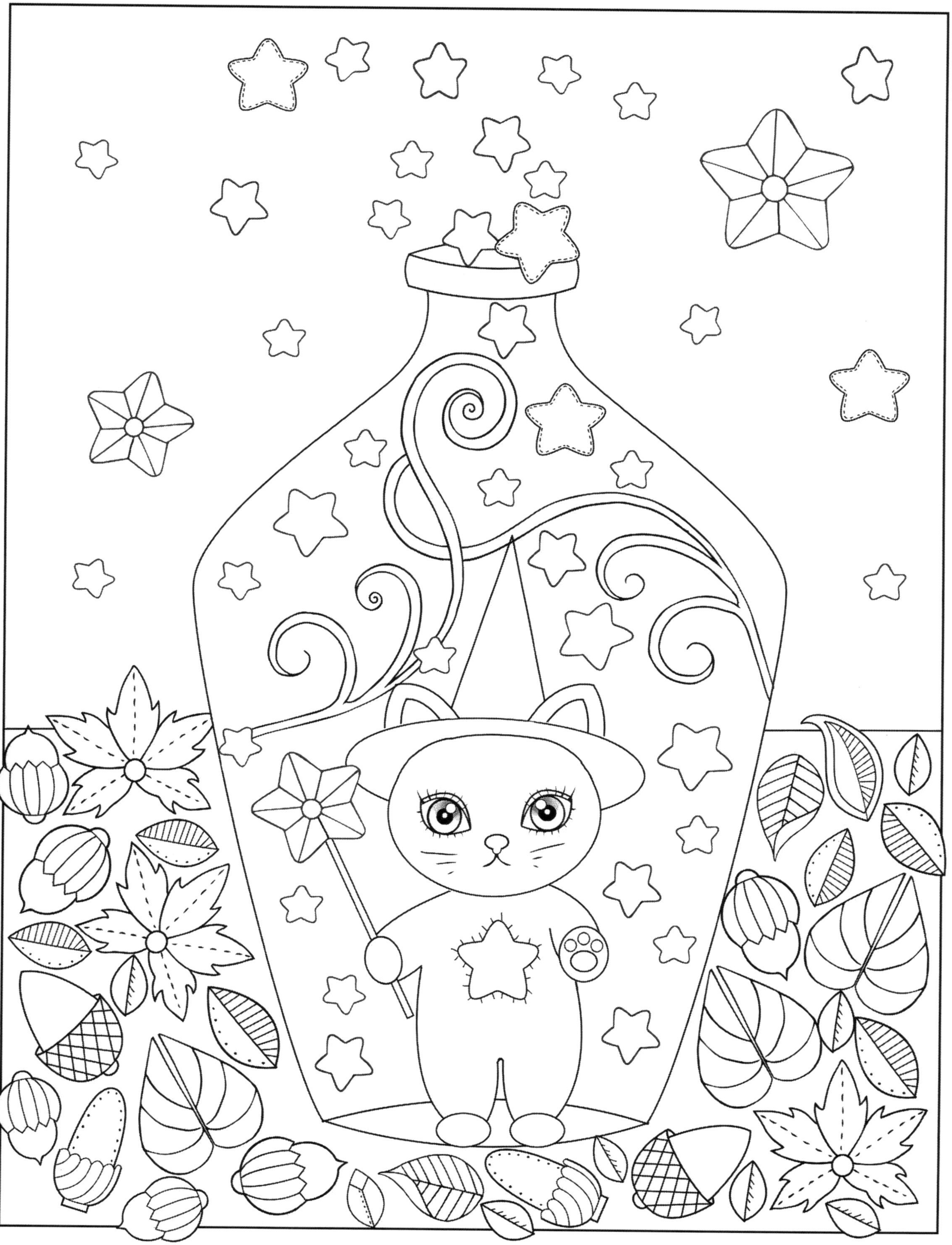

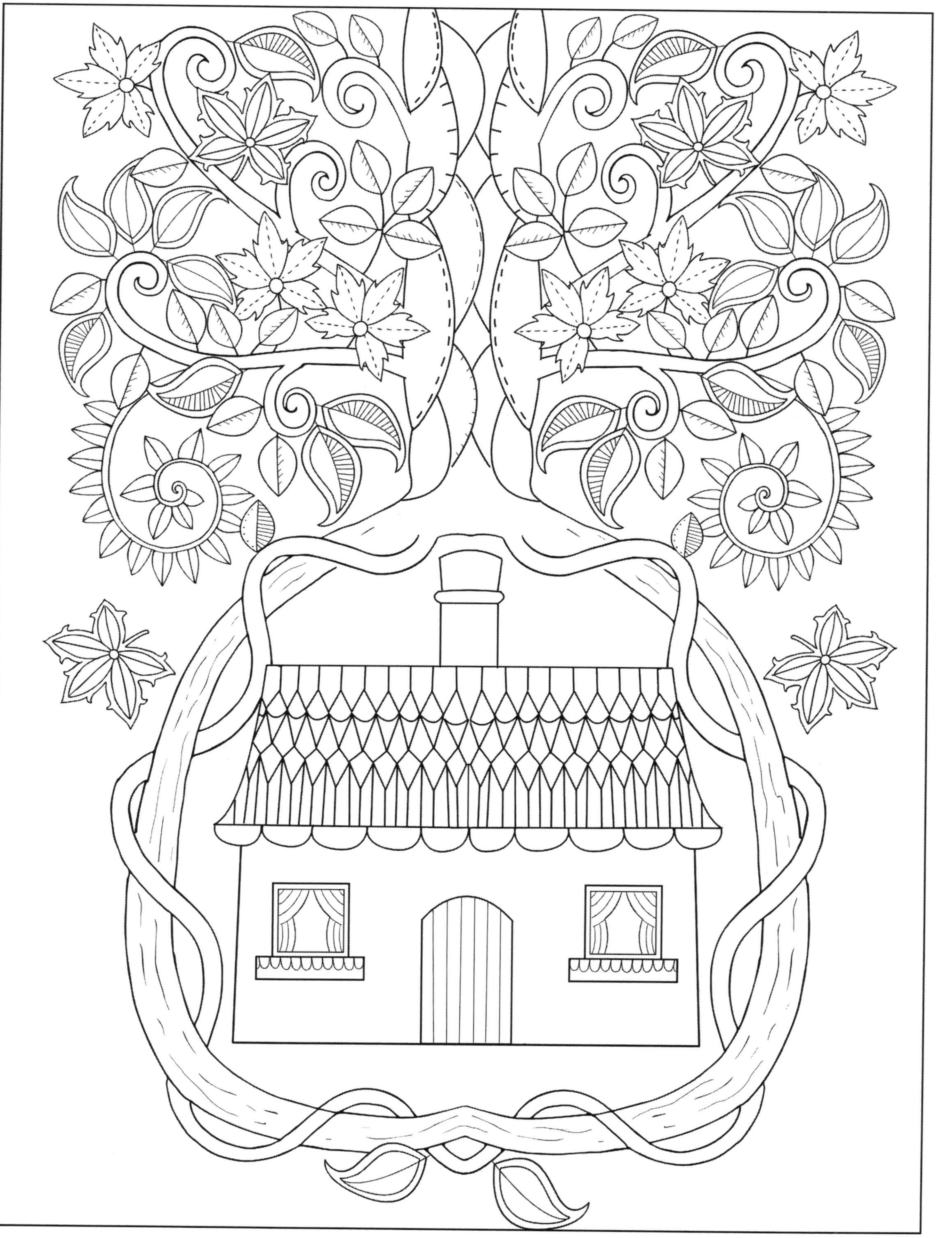

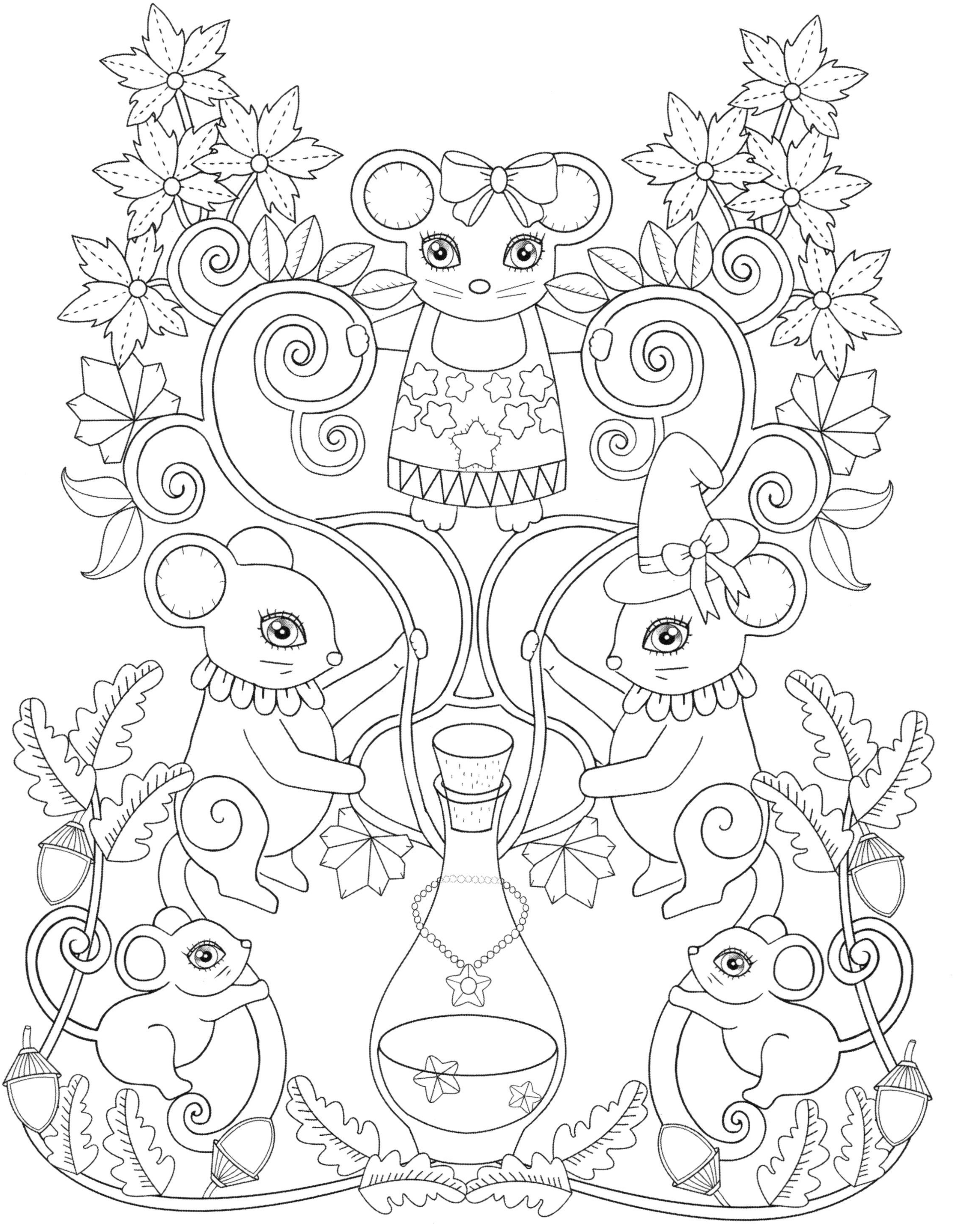

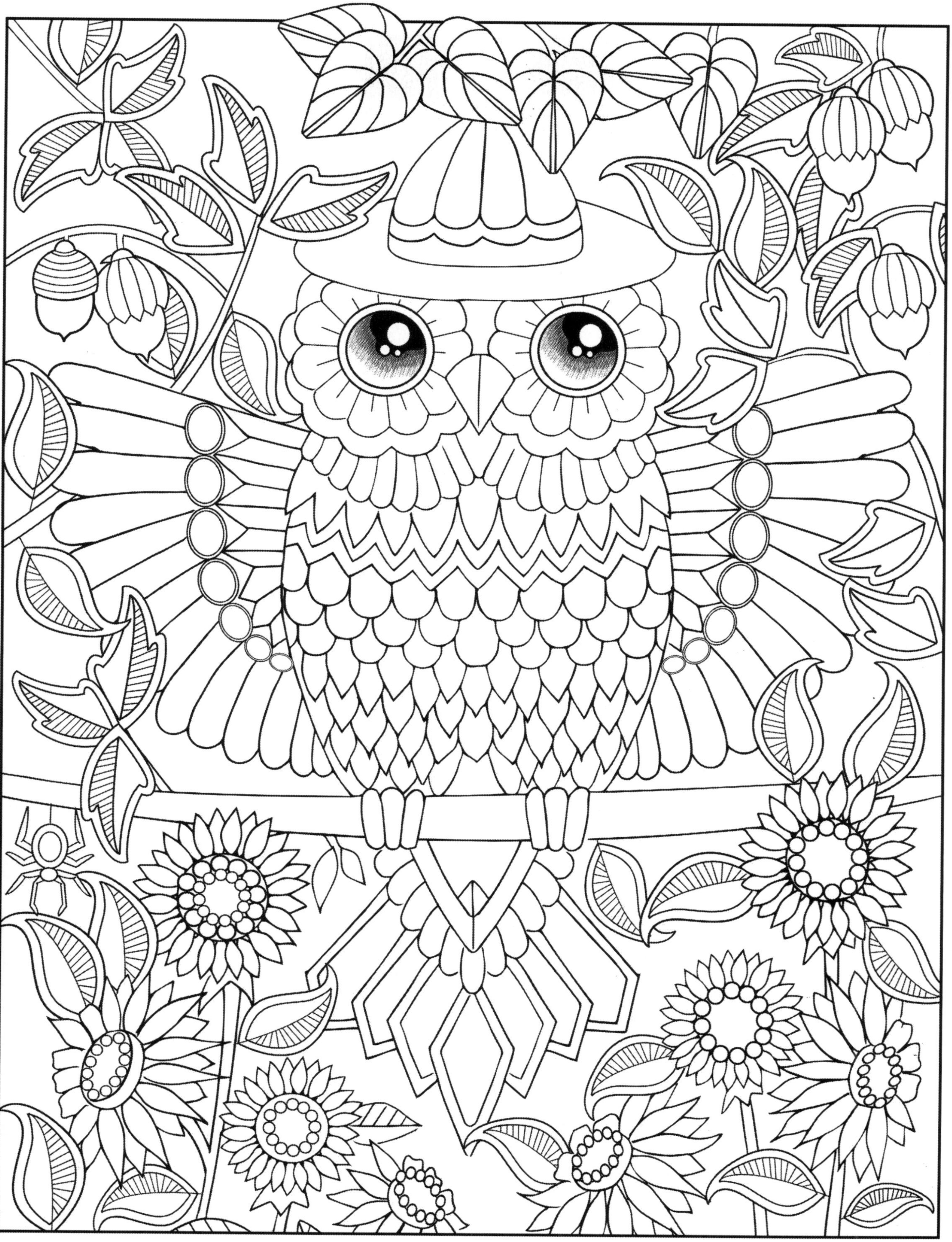

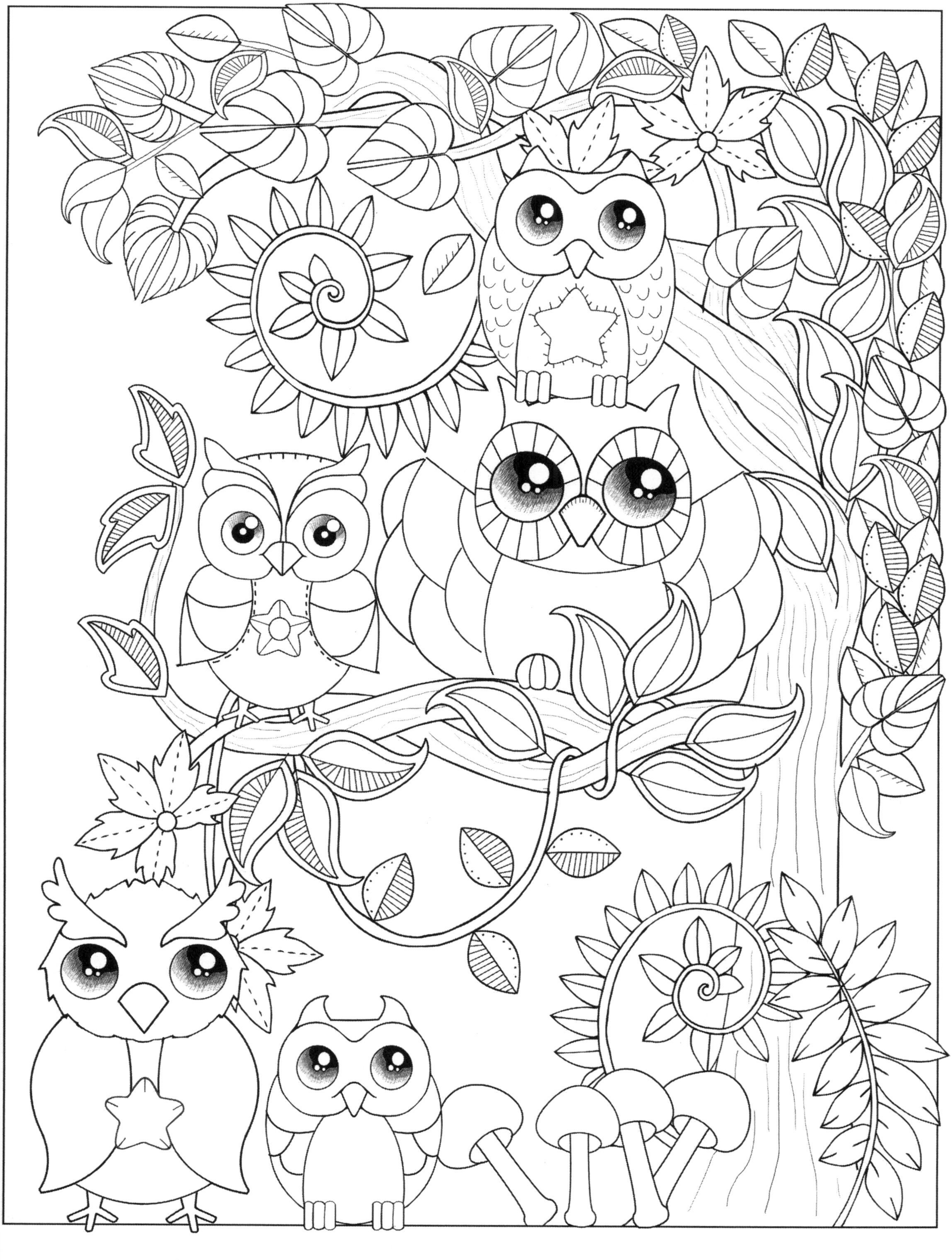

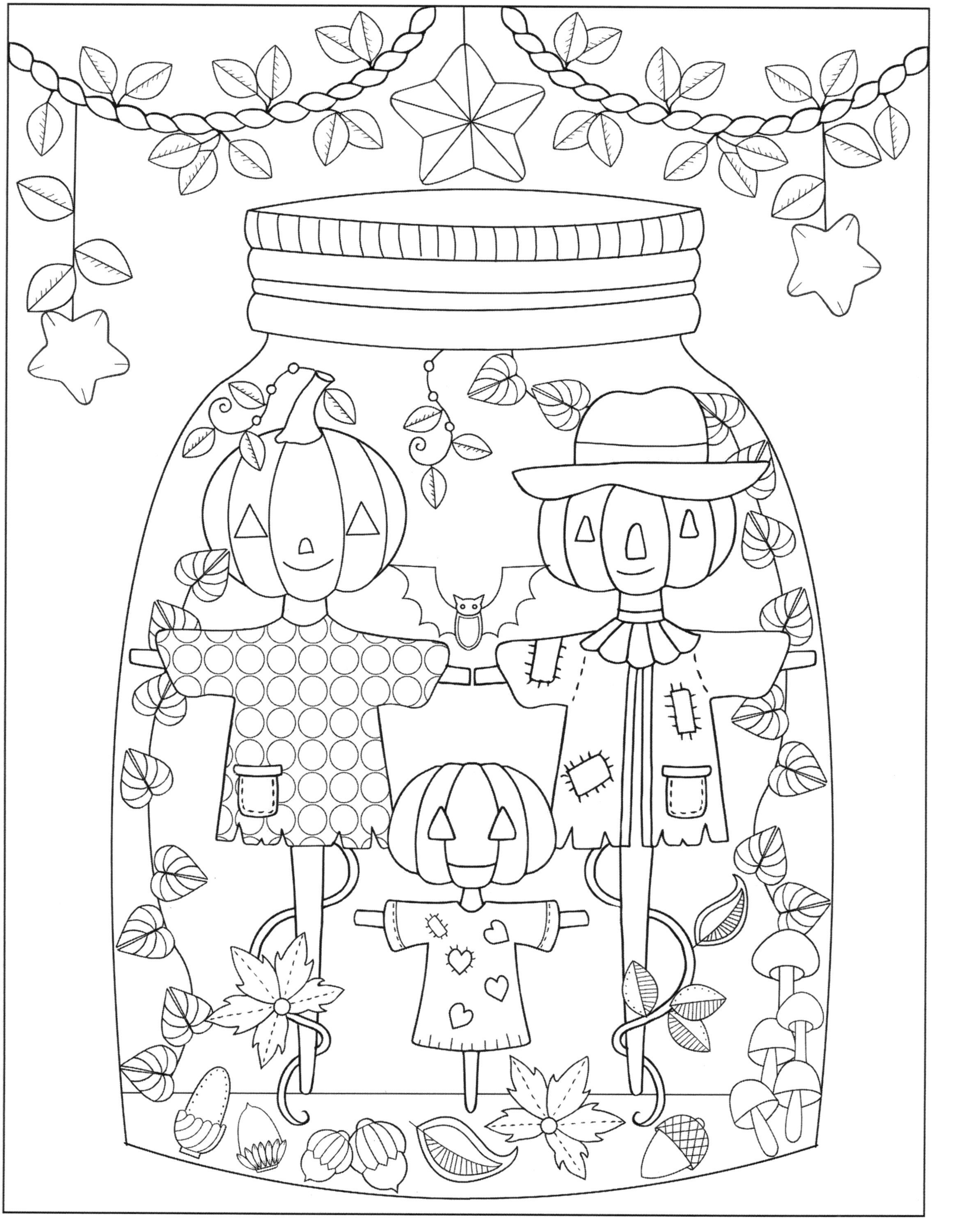

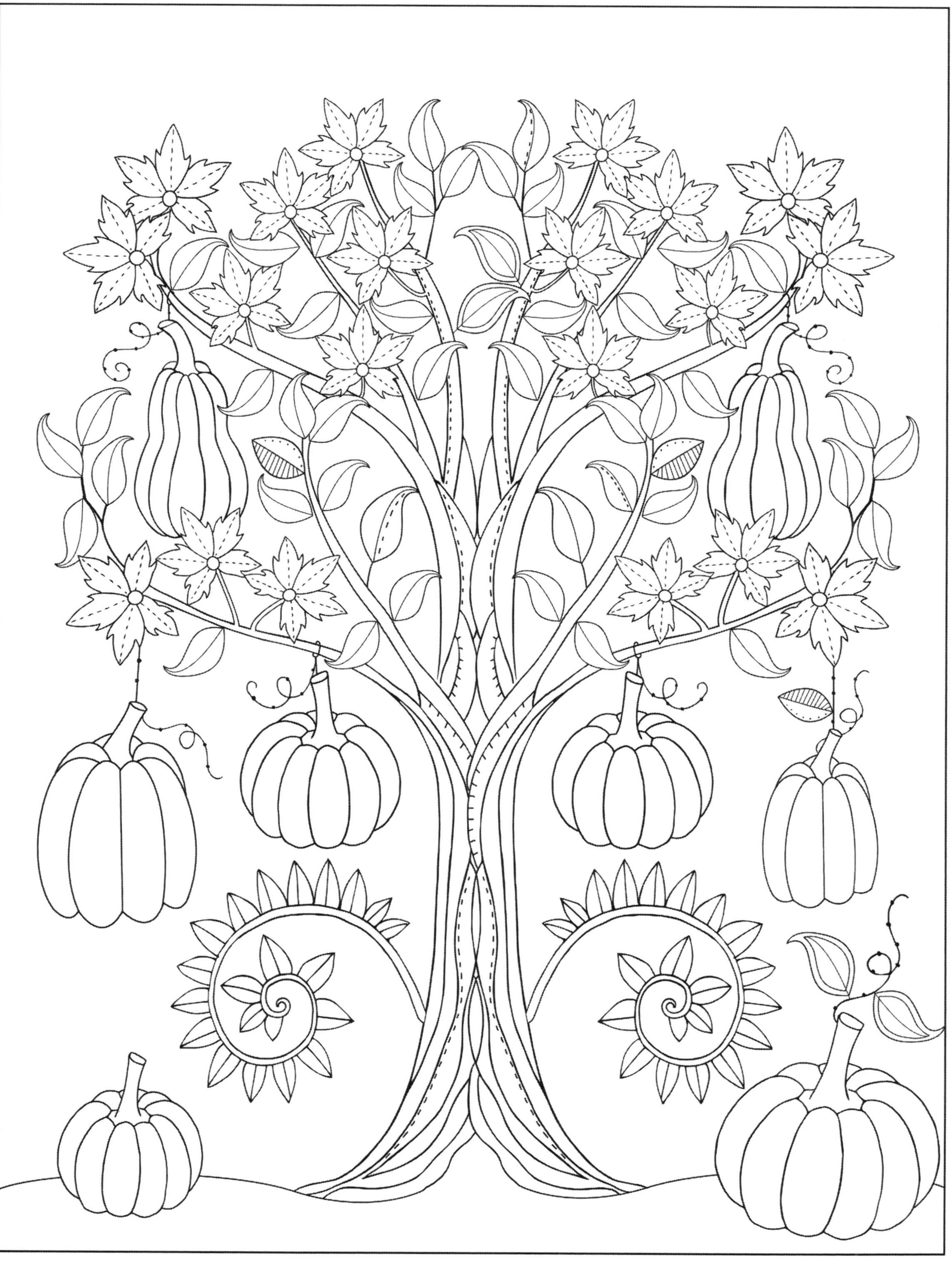

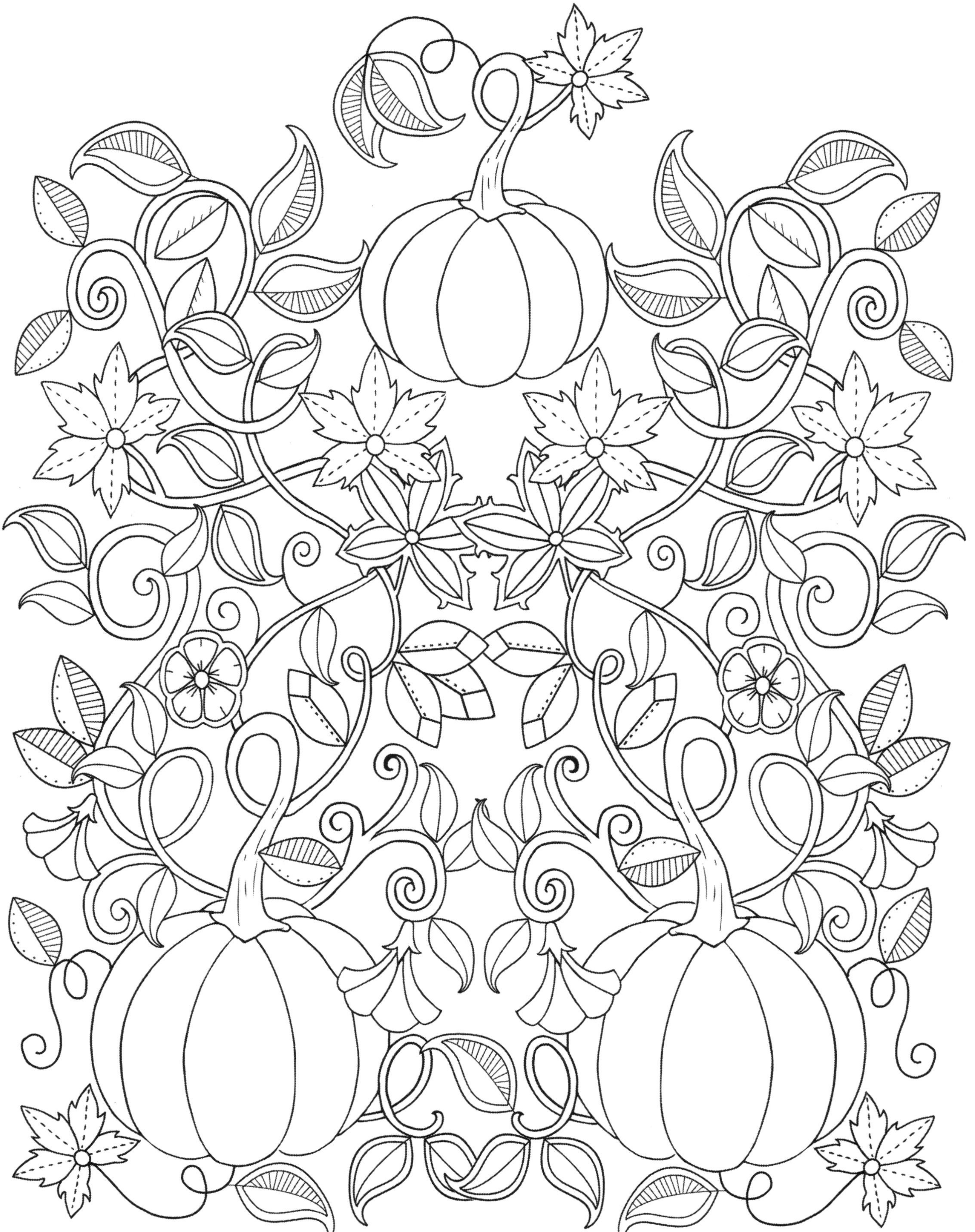

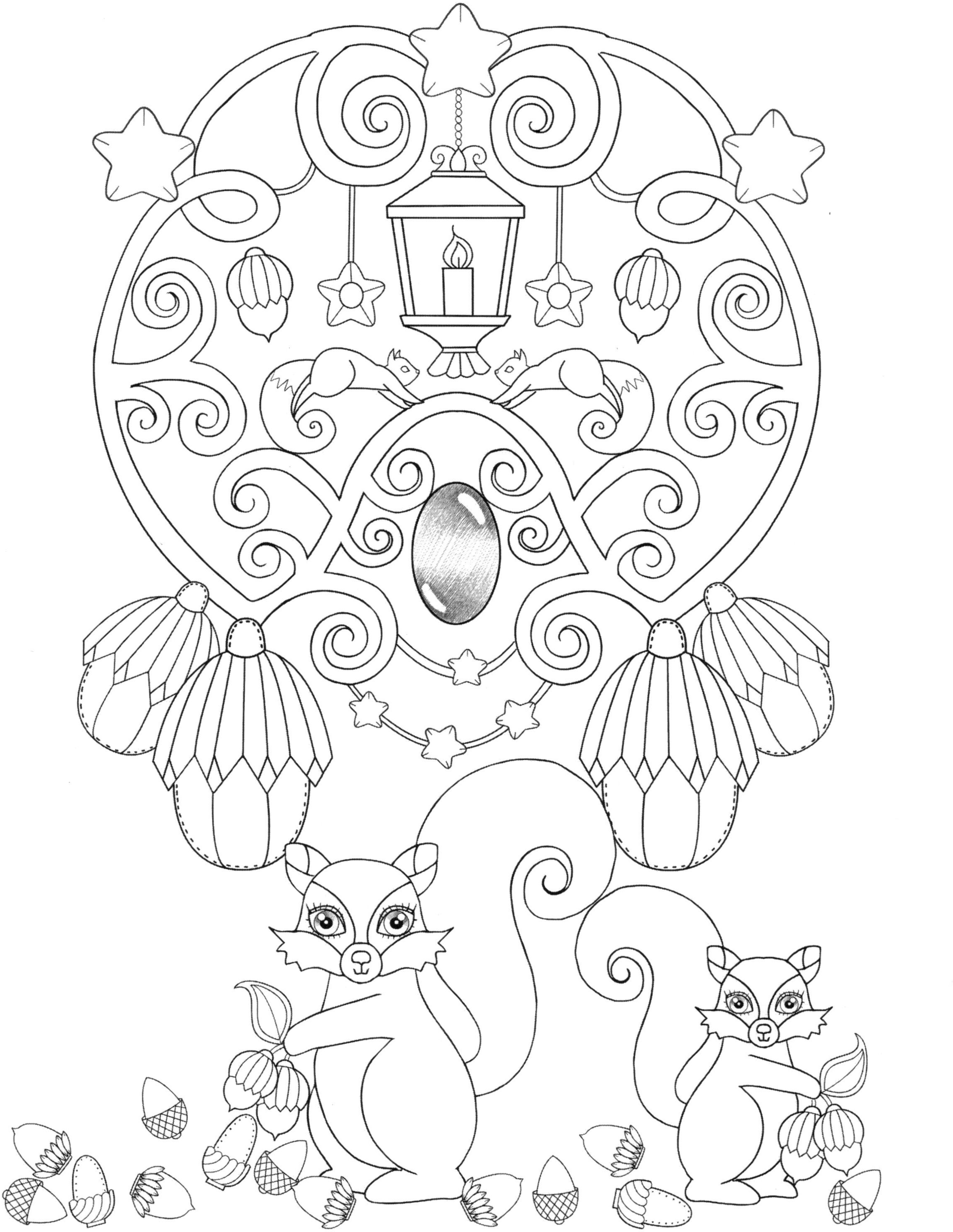

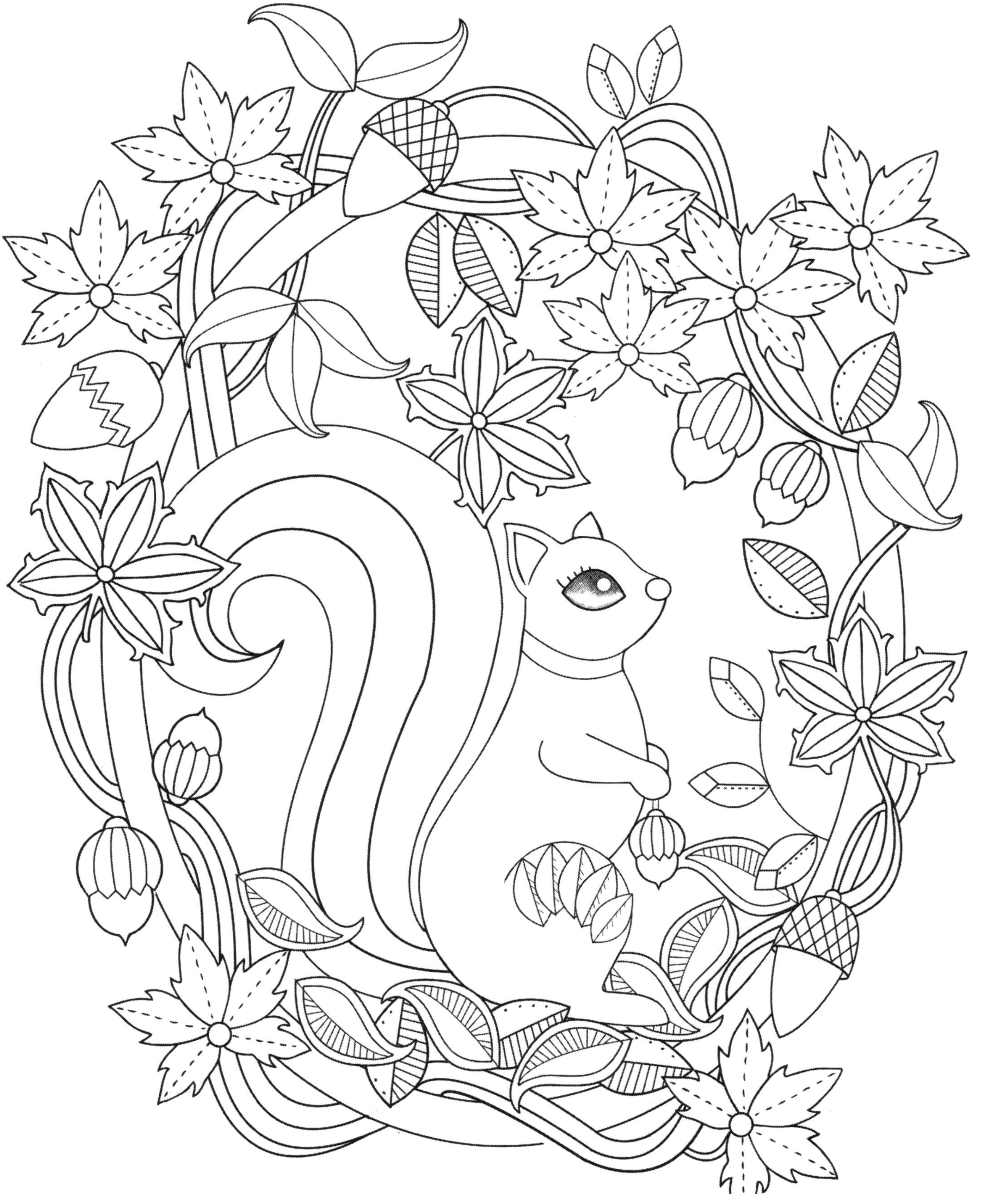

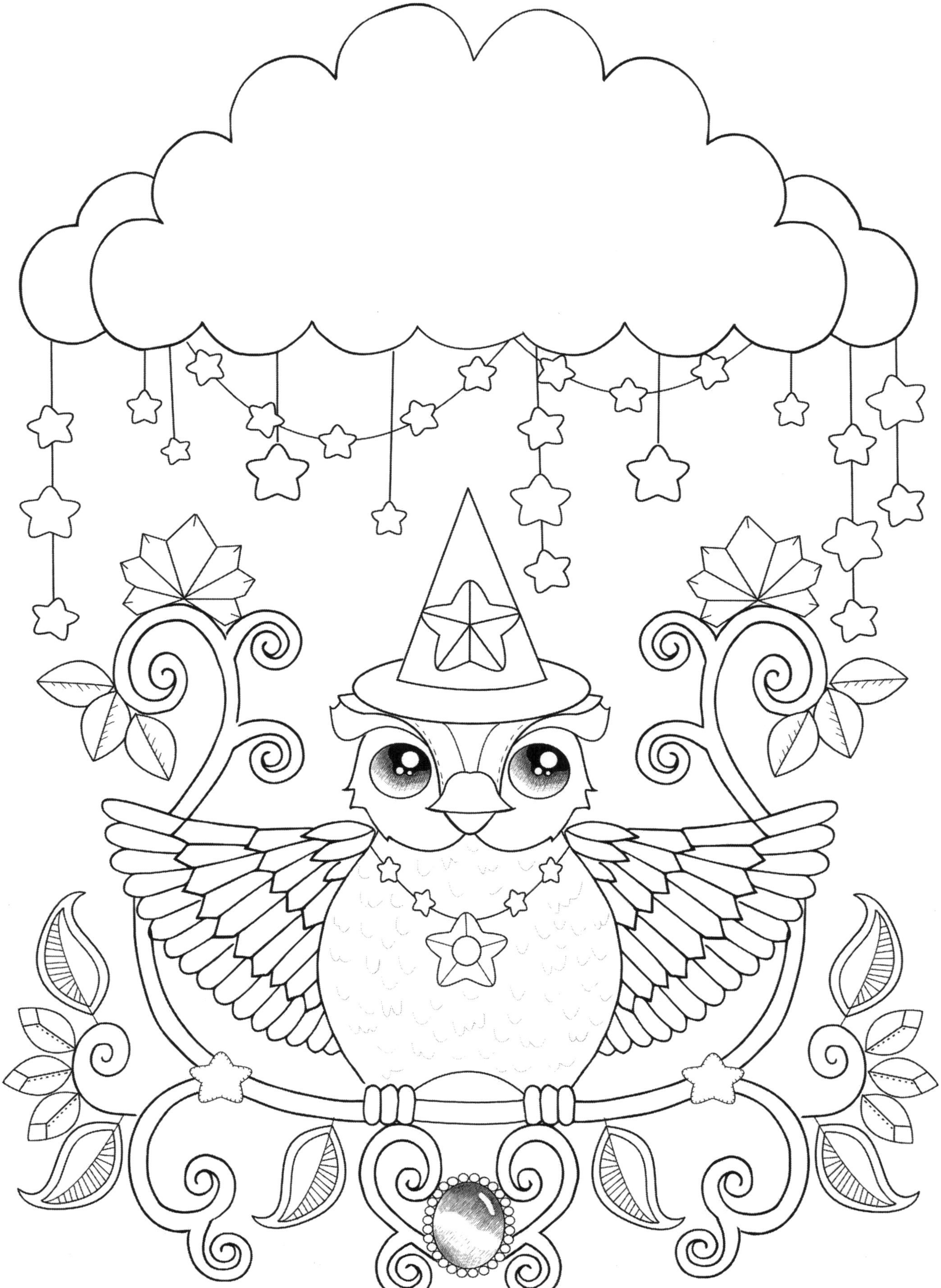

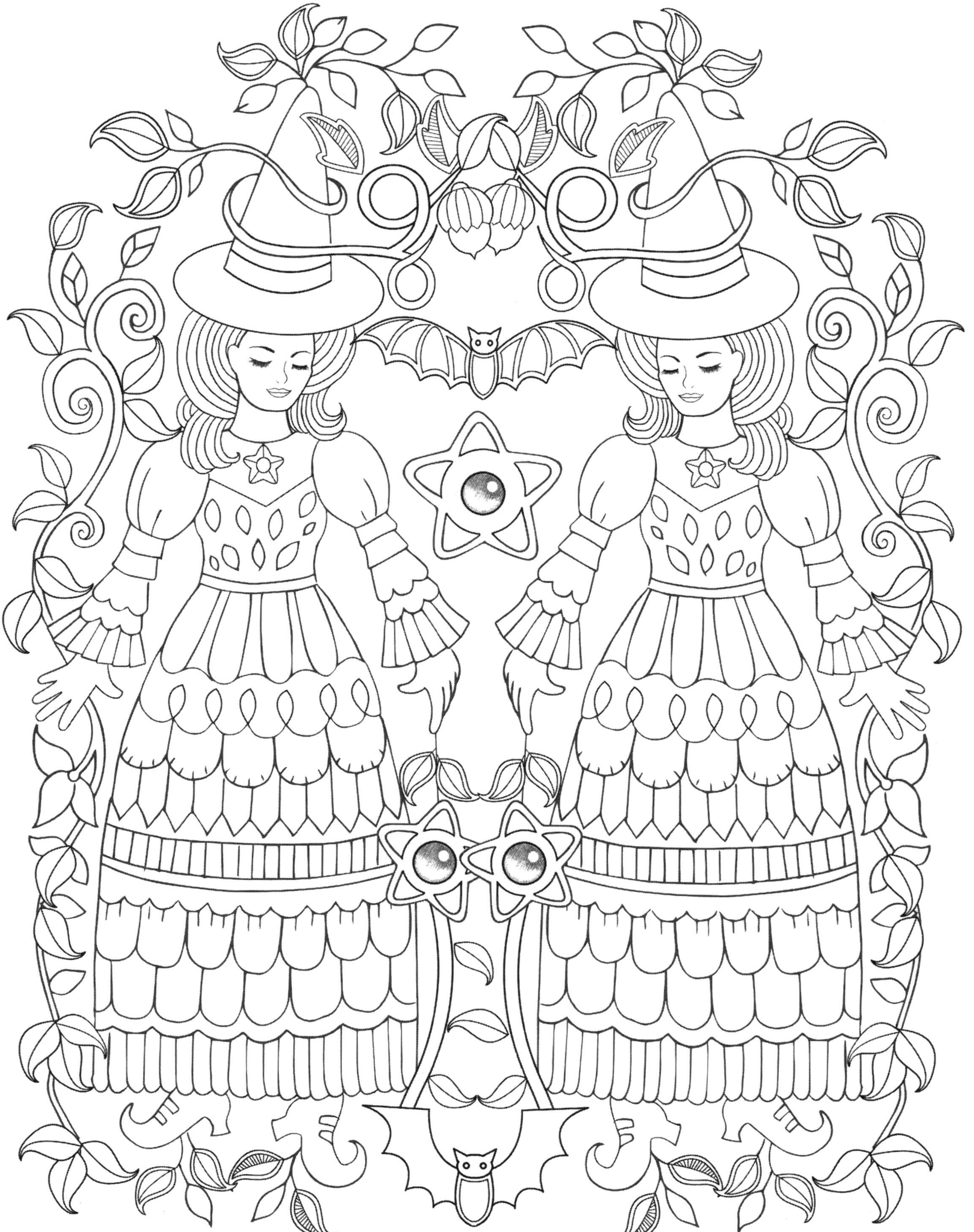

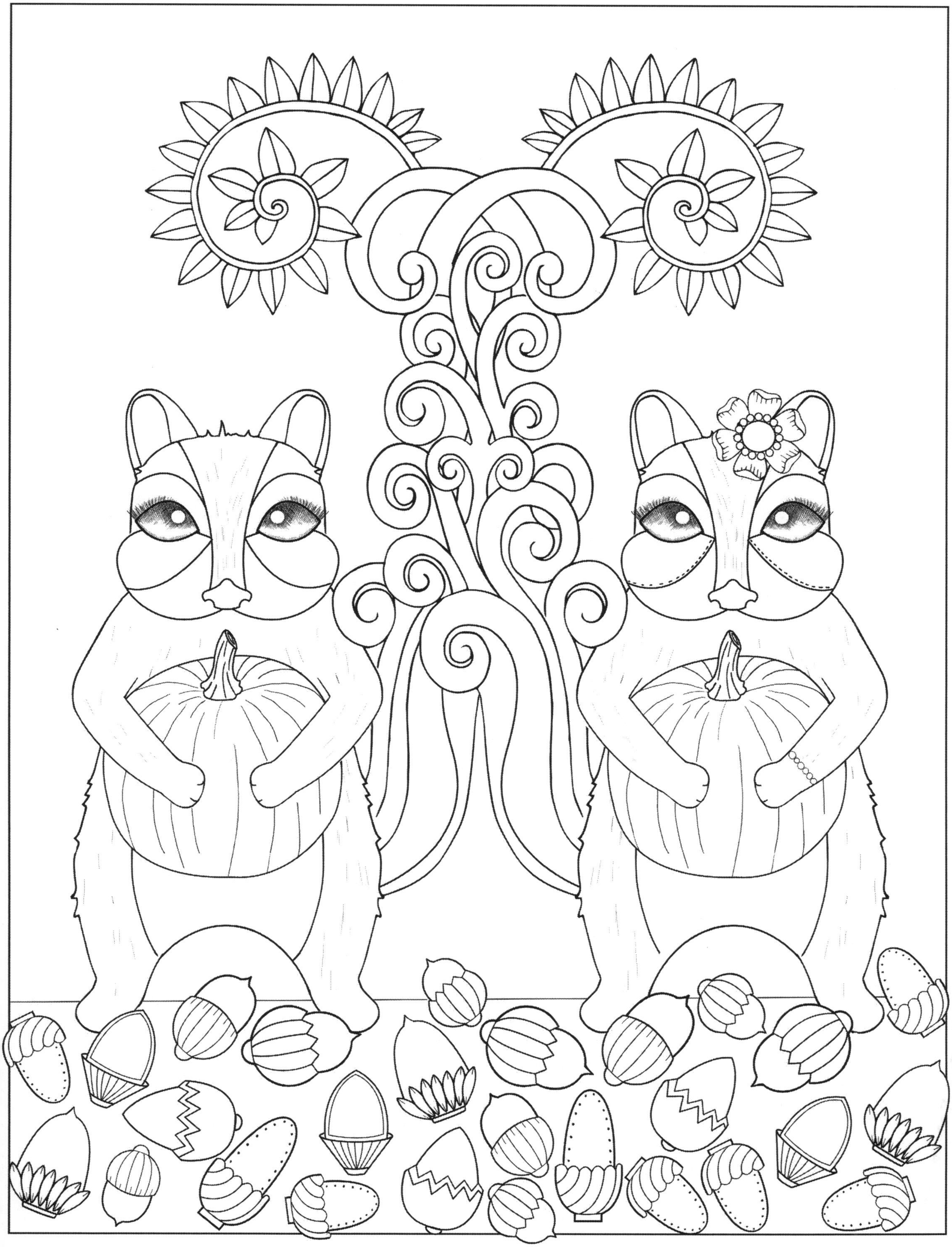

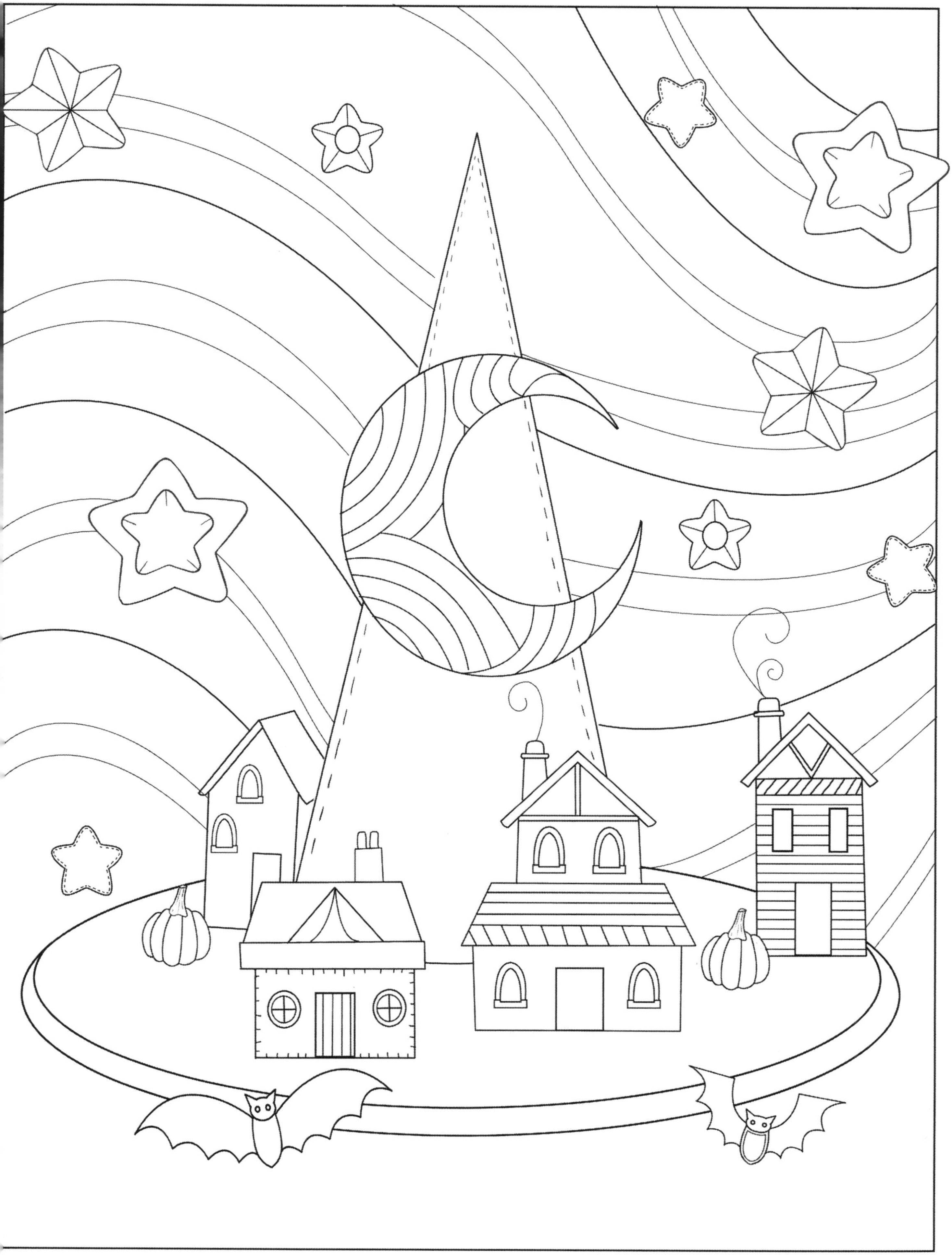

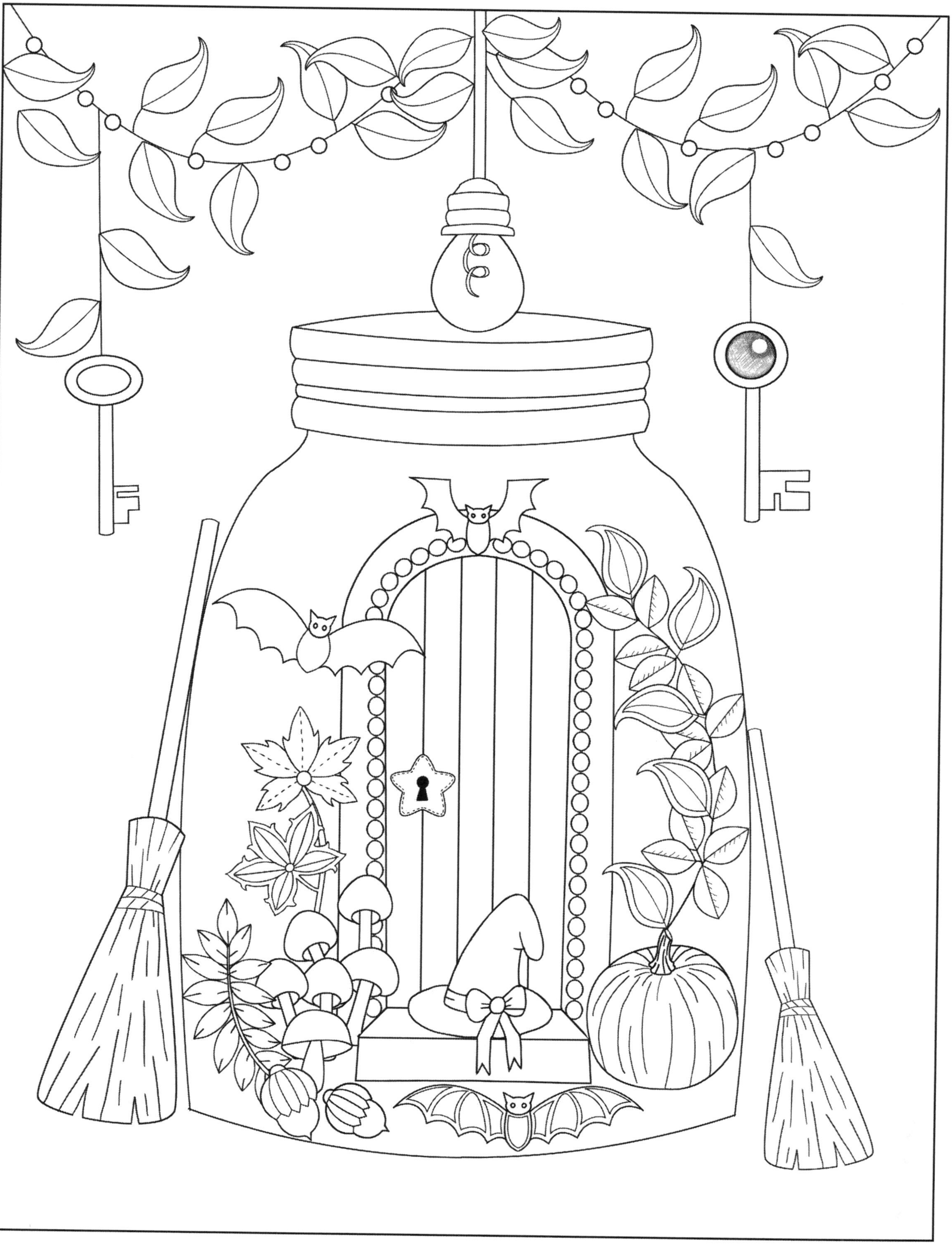

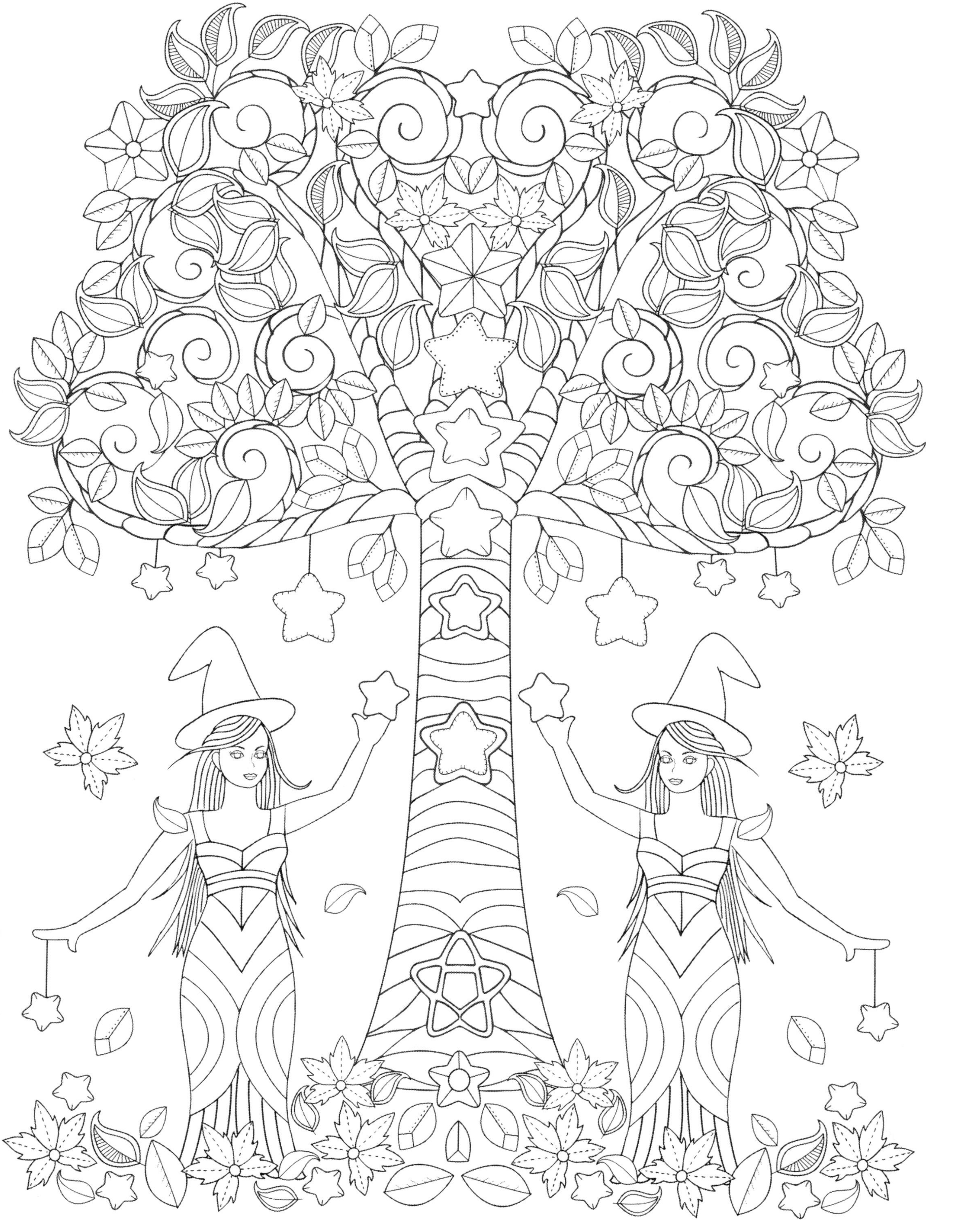

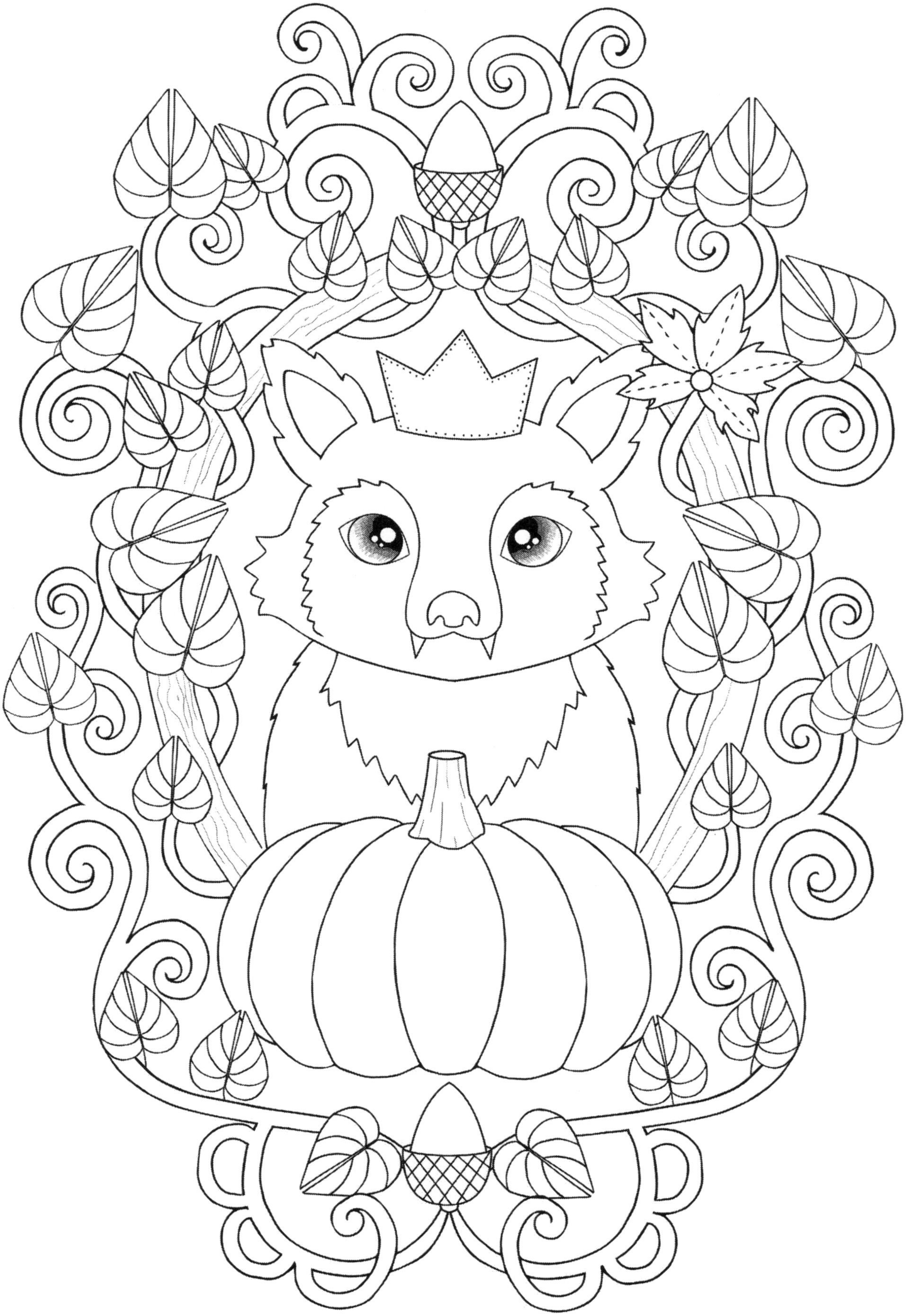

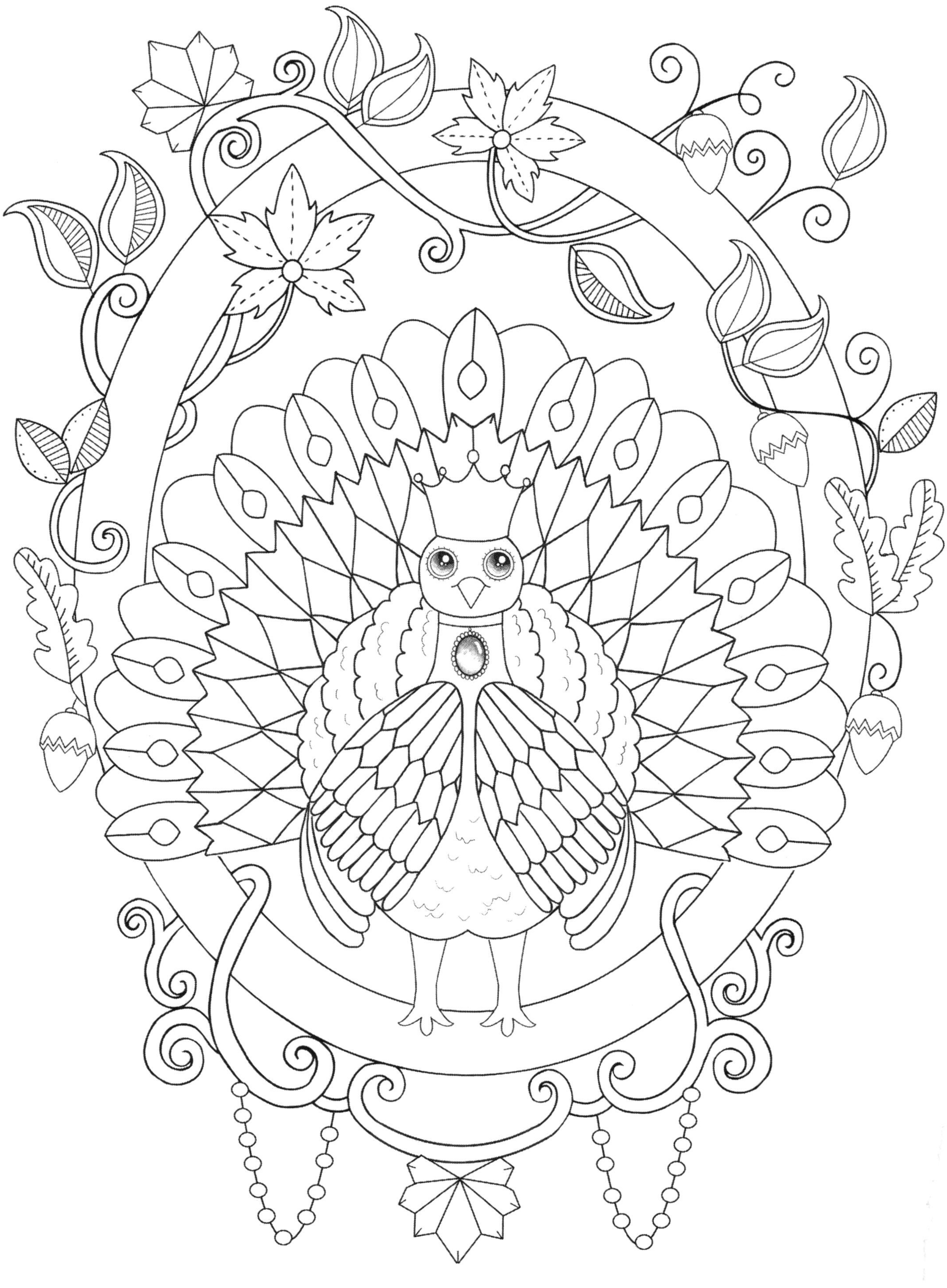

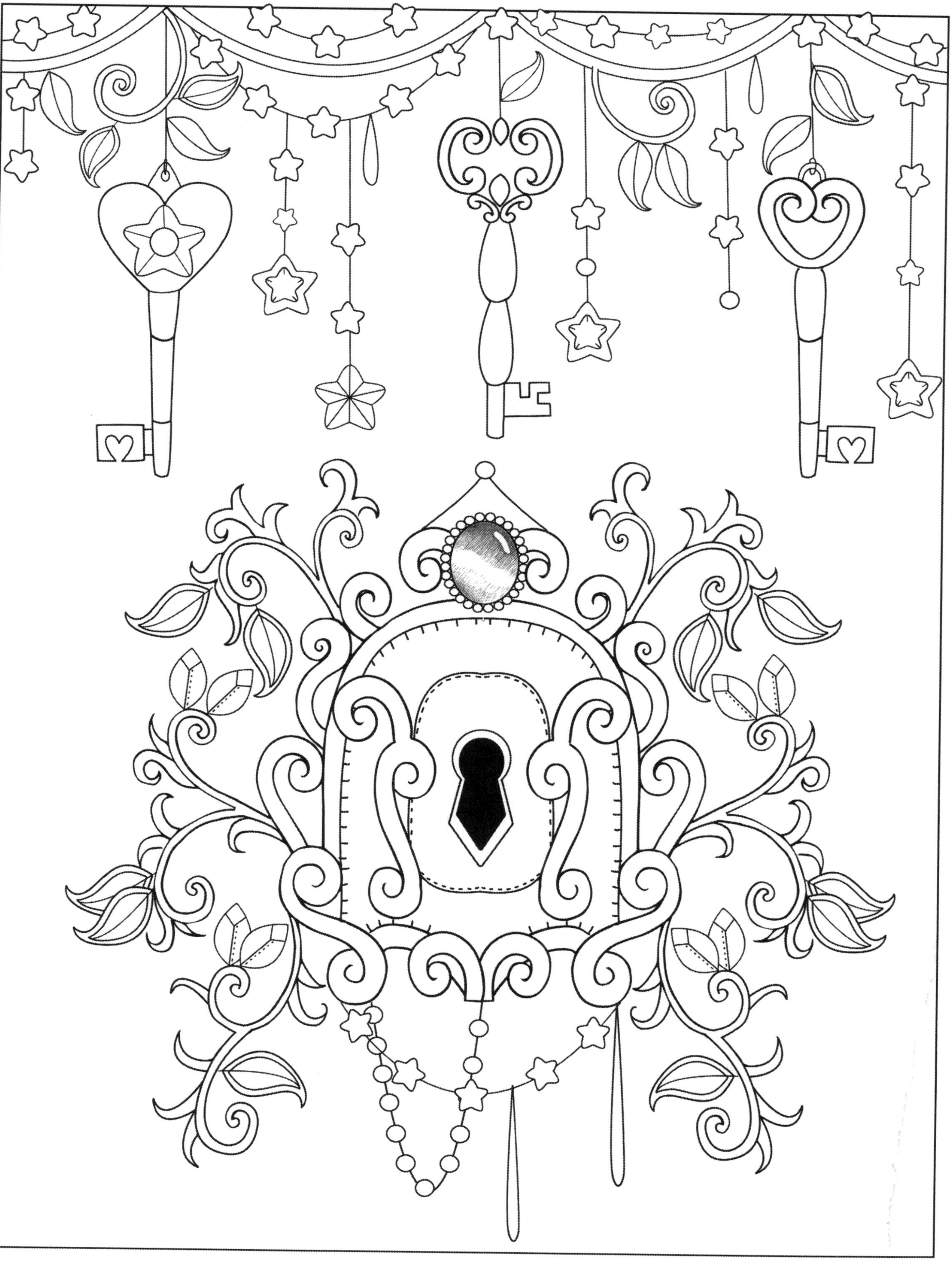

63217237R00037

Made in the USA
Lexington, KY
30 April 2017